THE ELEMENTS OF PREACHING

THE ELEMENTS OF PREACHING

WARREN WIERSBE
DAVID WIERSBE

Tyndale House
Publishers, Inc.
Wheaton, Illinois

Scripture quotations are from the King James Version
unless otherwise indicated.

Library of Congress Catalog Card Number 85-51839
ISBN 0-8423-0757-5

*To the faithful
multitude of people
who have enjoyed
and endured sermons,
week after week,
and still continue
to listen.*

Thank you!

CONTENTS

Preface 9

Part I. PREACHING PRINCIPLES 13
  1. Communicating God's Truth 17
  2. The Preacher and the Message 19
  3. Preaching As Worship 21
  4. Intent and Content 23
  5. Clarity 25
  6. Organization 29
  7. Essentials Not Accidentals 32
  8. The Outline 34
  9. Being Specific 35
 10. The Obvious and the Unexplainable . . . 37
 11. The Text and Its Reception 40
 12. Using Time Wisely 42
 13. Expression Not Impression 44
 14. Preaching Beneath the Surface 46
 15. Your Own Message 48
 16. Variety and Balance 50
 17. Planning to Preach 52
 18. Sermon Series 55
 19. Preaching to Individuals 57
 20. Doctrine, Duty, and Devotion 58
 21. Speaking the Truth 61
 22. Faith in Preaching 62
 23. Imagination 63
 24. Being Positive 65
 25. Preaching in the Present Tense 66
 26. Improving Preaching 68

Part II. PREACHING PROHIBITIONS 71
  1. Long Introductions 75
  2. Suppositions Rather Than Scripture . . . 79
  3. Poor English and Bad Grammar 81
  4. Hiding Behind the Pulpit 83
  5. Lecturing 84
  6. Careless Illustrations 86
  7. Overpowering Vocabulary 88
  8. Careless Delivery 90
  9. Vague and General Conclusions 92
 10. Verse Jumping 95
 11. Changing Translations 96
 12. Betraying Confidences 98
 13. Abusing Humor 100
 14. Preaching Ourselves 103

Taking Inventory of the Message 105
So, What's Cooking? 107

PREFACE

The dictionary defines "elements" as "the simplest principles of a subject of study." It is with this definition in mind that we have written this book. Our aim is to present simply and clearly the fundamentals of preaching.

This is not a book on how to prepare sermons. We now have more of these than we need. Nor is this a book advocating any special approach to preaching. Rather, our purpose is to spell out the basics that the preacher must grasp before he can adequately begin to use what the other books teach.

In short, we want this book to be to preaching what *The Elements of Style*, by William Strunk, Jr., and E. B. White, is to writing. The emphasis is on the fundamentals.

We have read and discussed numerous books on preaching, and, we think, benefited from them. We have listened to preachers and have preached a few sermons ourselves. The senior member of this team even dared to teach preaching in the seminary classroom!

Our conclusion is that the multitude of books, seminars, cassettes, lectures, and "preaching helps" gives the impression that preaching must be a complicated and burdensome task. We hope to convince you that, while preaching is not easy, its elements are really quite simple, and the application of them can bring real joy to your heart.

We agree with Phillips Brooks, who said in his Yale *Lectures on Preaching*, "For my part, I am startled when I think how few and simple are the things which I have to say to you. The principles which one can recognize in his ministry are very broad and plain. The applications of these principles are endless. . . ."

We also agree with the good Bishop when he said: "Let us rejoice with one another that in a world where there are a great many good and happy things for men to do, God has given us the best and happiest, and made us preachers of His Truth."

Amen and amen!

Happy preaching!

Warren W. Wiersbe
David W. Wiersbe

Note: References to, and quotations from, the great preachers must not be taken as endorsements of all that they believed, preached, or published. They are quoted or referred to because they have a specific contribution to make to the points in our book.

I. Preaching Principles

Methods are many,
Principles are few.
Methods always change,
Principles never do.

—Anonymous

Once we had golden ministers and wooden vessels; now we have wooden ministers and golden vessels.

—John Trapp

I preached as never sure to preach again, and as a dying man to dying men.

—Samuel Rutherford

Thou art a preacher of the Word; mind thy business!

—Old Puritan

Brethren, avoid anything like trifling over sermon-making.

—Charles Haddon Spurgeon

1. Preaching is the communicating of God's truth by God's servant to meet the needs of people.

If we accept this definition, we are making several important affirmations.

> There is such a thing as God's truth.
>
> We can know this truth, experience it, and share it with others.
>
> People can receive this truth, apply it, and be changed by it.

We are also accepting some serious obligations.

> We must know God's truth ourselves.
>
> We must experience the truth personally.
>
> We must know the people we minister to so that we may better apply the truth to their needs.
>
> We must diligently learn how best to communicate the truth to others.

We must grow in our love for truth and
our knowledge of it, so that our ministry might increase in depth and effectiveness.

2. The preacher is a part of the message.

Phillips Brooks defined preaching as "the bringing of truth through personality" *(Lectures on Preaching,* p. 5). The preacher is not only a herald, but also a witness. He has personally experienced the power of God's truth in his own life and therefore can share it with others.

The incarnation of Christ is evidence that God mediates his truth through human personality. "And the Word was made flesh and dwelt among us . . ." (John 1:14). As the preacher grows, so grows the message, and so grows the church. It is not enough to have the authority of the Word behind the sermon; one must also evidence the power of a life lived under the authority of that Word.

This explains why the preacher suffers: God is teaching him new lessons of faith for the encouragement of his people. It also explains why the preacher must cultivate his own personal walk with the Lord. The pulpit is no place for borrowed blessings. They must flow out of the minister's fellowship with God in order to be fresh and exciting.

In other words, the preacher as well as the sermon must be prepared. The two go together. In every part of his being—physical, mental, emotional, spiritual—the preacher must be a prepared vessel to contain, and then to share, the message of life. What God has joined together, let not preachers put asunder.

3. Preaching is an act of worship.

If it is not, then it will call attention to itself or to the preacher, and not to God. When preaching is not an act of worship, there is the danger that the congregation may worship the preacher and not God.

When a man has a high view of preaching, he will reach higher in his preaching. Paul looked upon his ministry as that of a priest at the altar: ". . . to be a minister of Christ Jesus to the Gentiles with the priestly duty of proclaiming the gospel of God, so that the Gentiles might become an offering acceptable to God, sanctified by the Holy Spirit" (Rom. 15:16, NIV).

If our preaching is an act of worship, we will want to give God our best. We will also seek to honor him, not glorify ourselves or try to show people how learned or clever we are. Furthermore, the sermon will then fit into the total context of worship so that everything in the service will point to the Savior.

"You can never make a sermon what it ought to be," said Phillips Brooks, "if you consider it alone. The service that accompanies it, the prayer and praise, must have their influence upon it" *(op. cit.*, p. 142).

4. A sermon must have both intent and content if it is to be effective.

The purpose of preaching is not simply to discuss a subject, but to achieve an object. A true sermon involves not only explanation but also application. A preacher must not be satisfied merely to instruct the mind; he must also stir the heart and motivate the will to apply God's truth personally.

An outline is not a message any more than a blueprint is a building or a recipe is a meal. What a sick man needs is medicine, not a lecture on health.

The object of the sermon will depend on several factors:

> The message of the text.
> The specific needs of the congregation.
> The particular burdens on the pastor's heart.

The leading of the Spirit of God as the minister meditates and prays.

The pastoral intent and the biblical content must not be divorced. G. Campbell Morgan once wrote in his diary this report of a message he listened to: "Heard a capital sermon with which I did not at all agree, on a text which had no relation to the subject." Even in Morgan's day, a text without a context was still a pretext!

5. The intent of the sermon must be made clear.

When the pilot does not know what port he is heading for, no wind is the right wind; and when the preacher does not know what he is trying to accomplish in his message, no service is a good service. Have a specific aim for each message, and be sure to tell your congregation what it is.

"A sermon ought to be a monograph and not an encyclopedia," said John Watson, "an agency for pushing one article, not a general store where one can purchase anything from a button to a coffin" *(The Cure of Souls*, p. 18).

If the preacher has done his heart-work and his homework, he should be able to state in one sentence exactly what his message is about and what he wants to accomplish. John Henry Jowett said, "I have a conviction that no sermon is ready for preaching . . . until we can express its theme in a short, pregnant sentence as clear as crystal" *(The Preacher: His Life and Work,* p. 133).

Teachers of homiletics call this sentence by different terms: the sermon proposition, the theme sentence, the "big idea." This sentence is to the sermon what the spine is to the skeleton, and the foundation to the house: it holds things together and helps to determine what the final product will become.

This proposition should have the following characteristics:

> It should be biblical, a timeless truth that is worth preaching about.
>
> It should be important and relevant to the needs of the congregation.
>
> It should be definite and clear, uncluttered by abstract language or literary embellishments.
>
> It should be accurate and honest and not promise more than the preacher can produce. You don't lay a foundation for a skyscraper and then build a chicken coop on it.
>
> It should be interesting so that the listener is encouraged to want to listen to the development of the theme in the sermon.

It should usually be stated in the present tense, what God does for us today and not what he did for Moses centuries ago. "Jesus helped Peter when he was sinking" is a valid statement; but for a sermon thesis, it would better be stated, "In the storms of your life, your Savior is present to help you."

Here are some additional examples:

If you really believe you are going to heaven, then that belief ought to make a difference in your life.

We usually think about the "blessings" of prayer; but have you ever considered prayer as dangerous business?

"The Lord God omnipotent reigneth!" Now, that cardinal conviction will be found, when you explore and examine it, to lead to three results.
—Dr. James S. Stewart

How does the Cross, with its message of forgiveness and healing, affect the memory of sin?
—Dr. William M. Clow

"What think ye of Christ?" Let us go to those who knew Christ, and ask what they thought of Him.
—Dwight L. Moody

What does it do for our prayers to conclude them with the words "through Jesus Christ our Lord"?
—Dr. Ralph W. Sockman

Here, then, are four reasons why people go to church.
—Dr. Leslie D. Weatherhead

Habakkuk, from his vantage point near to the heart of God, gains new insights for the warning of the wicked and the encouragement of the righteous.
—Dr. Charles W. Koller

That brings us to the vital issue. How does faith overcome doubt?
—Dr. Harry Emerson Fosdick

6. The sermon must be organized.

God is not the author of confusion, but some preachers are, and they do it in God's name. Whether the congregation identifies each point or sub-point in the outline is not that important. But the preacher must know where he is going and how to get there. Once the theme has been announced, there must be a *development* of the material in an interesting and practical way.

Most sermon outlines would consist of:
    An introduction
    A statement of purpose (proposition, "big idea")
    Two or more main points (development)
    Conclusion

The artist studies anatomy so that his painting of the human figure will be more realistic.

What the skeleton is to the body, the outline is to the sermon: it is not obvious, but it had better be there.

The structure of the sermon depends primarily on the development of the material in the biblical text. It is an unpardonable sin to develop an outline and then force it upon a passage of Scripture.

The structure also depends on the statement of purpose. In the examples given above, you can see how this works out. Dr. James Stewart's sermon will have three main points and each of them will be *a result*. Mr. Moody's sermon will have many points as he introduces the *persons* who knew Jesus. Dr. Weatherhead's sermon will have four main points and each will be a reason for attending church.

Finally, the structure should take into account the total "preaching pattern" of the minister. There is always a need for variety. The itinerant preacher can use the same homiletical approach because he changes congregations; but the resident pastor must change approaches because he speaks to the same congregation week after week. To use "reasons" or "results" or "lessons" every Sunday would make our preaching predictable and rob the message of power.

Each preacher has his own distinctive style, and this is as it should be. The beginning preacher would do well to submit himself to the disciplines of the homiletical rules until he has discovered and developed his own unique approach. You can break the rules once the rules have broken you.

Organization in a sermon must be a servant and not a master. The preacher must live with the same tension that the architect battles—form vs. function. "What a marvelous outline!" is not the highest compliment a preacher can receive. Far better for us to hear, "You showed us the Lord today, and he met our need."

7. The sermon should be based on the essentials of the text and not the accidentals of the translation you are using.

The preacher who preaches from Paul's three "ready" statements (Acts 21:13—"ready to die"; Rom. 1:15—"ready to preach"; and 2 Tim. 4:6—"ready to be offered") in the Authorized Version is heading for a homiletical hodgepodge. In the first text, the Greek word means "prepared"; while in the second, the word means "eager." Paul was not eager to die, but he was eager to preach! The word "ready" is not found at all in 2 Timothy 4:6. "I am already being offered" is the sense of the original. A clever outline ruined by good exegesis.

Preachers who are addicted to alliteration

like to find words in their text that begin with the same letter and somehow tie them together in an outline. Sometimes this approach will work (e.g., *flee*, *follow*, *fight*, in the KJV of 1 Tim. 6:11, 12), but usually it leads to a forced outline based on bad exegesis.

There is no substitute for a knowledge of the original languages to set you free from bondage to a translation. Many fine basic tools are available today so that even the person with little knowledge of Hebrew and Greek may secure the technical help needed.

The careful student of the Word will always consult several reliable translations, as well as the original, just to make certain he is on the main highway and not on a dangerous detour.

One test of the validity of the sermon outline is this: can you preach it from any reliable translation? If your outline is limited to one translation, then you may be building on the accidentals and not the essentials. One exception to this rule would be when a translation gives a unique coloring to a phrase or a verse, and you point this out to your listeners. Just be sure that, with all its uniqueness, the translation is still accurate.

8. Build your outline on the unique features of the text.

Many of the Psalms may be outlined in three points: trial, trust, and triumph. And several of the miracles follow this pattern: difficulty, faith, and victory. In many of Paul's admonitions you find the recurring pattern of doctrine, duty, and the resulting blessing (or "delight" if you are seeking to alliterate the outline). However, these points *describe* the character of the passage or the event; they do not interpret and apply the passage. This approach is helpful in analyzing a text but not in preaching it.

Almost every passage in the Bible could be preached with a four-point "outline": the setting, the wording, the meaning, and the living. These four points can give you a helpful analysis of a passage and assist you in finding its unique features, but they are a poor outline of a message.

9. Be specific.

Propagandists depend on glittering generalities, but preachers of the gospel must be specific. There is power and authority in precision.

The sermon proposition must be specific. "There are several things in this passage that should help us become better Christians" is the kind of sermon statement every preacher ought to avoid. In fact, the word "things" is vague and should be used with caution. What kind of "things" do we mean? Warnings? Obstacles? Encouragements? Then let's say so!

"Truths," "lessons," and "ideas" are also to be used with caution. The careful preacher will use his dictionary—especially his dictionary of synonyms—and will keep in mind Mark Twain's dictum that the difference between any word and the right word is the difference between lightning and a lightning bug. Chesterton said just about the same thing: "A man does not know what he is saying until he knows what he is not saying."

There is a difference, for example, between *results* and *consequences*, *difficulties* and *dilemmas*, *unity* and *uniformity*, *punishment* and *discipline*. The effective minister of the Word uses words the way a craftsman uses tools—the right word for the right job. "The Preacher sought to find delightful words and to write words of truth correctly" (Eccles. 12:10, NASB).

We should also be specific when it comes to names, dates, and statistics. Do some research and get accurate figures. The precise date carries far more power than "a few years ago," and the precise figure means much more than "a couple of hundred people were killed."

Be specific in Bible references and quotations, and be sure you check *every reference* before you finalize your outline. Even concordances can contain typographical errors, and books of sermons often perpetuate them.

Clear preaching must begin with clear thinking. Give yourself time to think through the text, the purpose, and the development of the message. Avoid fuzzy thinking and aim for precision.

10. Don't try to explain either the obvious or the unexplainable.

Laboring the obvious bores people, and trying to explain the unexplainable irritates them. There is mystery to the Christian faith and not everything in life or in the Bible can be explained. God does not contradict himself, but his ways are above our ways and we cannot always fathom his thoughts. Wise is the preacher who knows how to preach suggestively when the text will not permit him to preach exhaustively.

At the same time, never assume that your listeners know more about things spiritual than they really do. Spiritual illiteracy abounds. If you think a text needs it, sketch the historical background simply and quickly. You will remind the learned and educate the unlearned without cluttering your message.

We labor the obvious by explaining or illustrating that which everybody already knows. "Be honest at all times!" said one preacher we heard. "Be honest to your father and mother, because they brought you into the world. Be honest to your brothers and sisters, because you must live with them. Be honest to your friends. Be honest to your fellow-workers, and be honest to your neighbors. In every area of life, be honest—at home, in school, in church, at work, in the neighborhood." We got the impression that he had forgotten his next point and was in a boring holding-pattern, looking for the right runway.

Another minister, illustrating James 3:8 ("But the tongue can no man tame"), said: "I remember going to the circus as a lad and admiring the tamed animals. There were the tigers that had been tamed, and there were the lions that had been tamed. The tigers and lions jumped on the stools, jumped through the fiery hoops, and obeyed the man with the gun and the chair. Then there were the tamed elephants. What a marvel that these huge creatures would walk behind each other, each holding the other's tail. They were tamed! Then the clowns came in with the tamed dogs, fluffy white dogs that walked on their hind legs, walked on a tightrope, and even danced together. They were tamed!"

The problem is, he had so tamed his congregation that they were no longer listening to him. Repetition had become redundancy.

"What is so tedious as a twice-told tale?" asked Homer in his *Odyssey*. We really don't mind a twice-told tale if the teller has the skill to make it sound new each time it is told.

11. Keep your preaching within the bounds of what the text says and what the people can receive.

The saints are human and can assimilate only so much truth at one time. The larger the congregation, the greater the variety of needs and levels of spiritual growth. As you prepare your message, visualize "representative people" in the congregation—the confused teenager, the young couple, the lonely widow, the unemployed father—and prepare as though you were personally addressing them.

Sufficient for each text is the truth thereof; there is usually no need to chase all over the Bible for additional ideas. If such homiletical helter-skelter is necessary, perhaps your text is too brief and you ought to expand it.

Good preachers own wastebaskets and use

them. They realize that not every choice idea can be worked into the message, lest the sermon become a monstrosity. If your propositional sentence is clear and accurate, you will know which ideas to use and which ones to set aside for another time.

Better that our people get ahold of one or two meaty truths and put them to good use, than that they become lost in a maze of sermonic material and have nothing to show for it.

After completing his preparation, the preacher should do what accomplished writers and editors do: he should look at the material and ask himself, "So what?" What difference will it make in anybody's life if this sermon is preached? If your response is neutral, go back to the drawing board. Are you preaching because you have to say something, or because you have something to say?

12. Use your preaching time wisely.

In planning public ministry, everybody usually tries to give priority to the preaching of the Word from the pulpit; but we don't always succeed. The service may begin late, the prelude may take longer, and perhaps the announcements got out of hand.

Or, you may be a guest preacher having absolutely no control over the program schedule. At any rate, for one reason or another, your preaching time is limited. What do you do?

You do not complain. Just preach a good message and the congregation will do the complaining because you didn't have sufficient time.

You do not refer to matters you would like to discuss if you had the time. That just wastes more time!

You get right into your message as though you had the whole day at your disposal; but as you preach, you abandon the low-priority items in the message and focus on the important matters. If your message is well prepared, you can do this and nobody will know the difference.

A sermon does not have to be eternal to be immortal. Be thankful for the opportunity to minister the Word in love. Remember: the entire Sermon on the Mount can be read aloud in less than ten minutes.

13. Preach to express, not to impress.

If the purpose of preaching is to meet human needs, then that preacher is an impertinent thief who uses the pulpit to show off his homiletical or oratorical skills. Like John the Baptist, the preacher must decrease while the Savior increases (John 3:30). Jesus is the Word; the preacher is only the voice.

There ought to be such simplicity about our preaching that people will say to themselves, "I could have preached that sermon." True art always hides itself.

George H. Morrison was right: "Preach, not for the salvation of your sermon, but for the salvation of souls." Don't strive to prepare and preach "great sermons" but to magnify a great Savior. Always work harder and aim higher, but deliver yourself of the burden of preaching "great sermons." God's standards of measurement are usually different from ours.

If you use theological terms, be sure you explain them clearly. A simple word is preferred to a technical term, and a concrete word to one that is abstract. Profundity is not born of complexity; it is born of simplicity.

14. Preach beneath the surface.

To begin with, preach beneath the surface of the text. To paraphrase the words of the text is not the same as preaching the truths in the words. Spurgeon said that he used to "soak himself in the text," and that's a good idea. Ask yourself these questions:

> What does the text say? (facts, information)
>
> What does the text mean? (truths, interpretation)
>
> What does the text mean *to me?* (illumination and application)
>
> How can I make it meaningful to others? (imagination, organization)

You should also preach to reach below the surface of the listener. Never be satisfied unless the Spirit applies the Word to hearts and people respond in one way or another. Their response may even be negative! Paul's synagogue messages turned some people into converts and others into scoffers or enemies.

Finally, preach beneath your *own* surface, and be sure you feel the message deep within you. Don't "build a sermon" the way a carpenter builds a table, by gathering pieces from here and there and nailing them together. The message must be a *living* entity. It must grow out of the soil of your soul, and its roots must come from deep within your own experience and your study of God's Word. Sermons that are assembled from bits and pieces of other men's productions usually sound manufactured rather than cultivated. They are verbal essays, but not vital messages; they are not truth communicated through dedicated personality.

"Often, I'm afraid, the church is a place where preachers preach not out of their depths, but out of their shallows" (Frederick Buechner, *A Room Called Remember,* Harper & Row, 1984, p. 123).

15. Preach your own message.

This means the message God has given you, presented in the way he wants you to present it.

Plagiarism has been defined as the lowest form of larceny and the highest form of compliment. Dean Inge called originality "undetected plagiarism." The faithful preacher will milk a great many cows, but he will make his own butter. Mark Twain was right: "Adam was the only man who, when he said a good thing, knew that nobody had said it before him."

You need not document every truth or idea in your sermon that you picked up from your studies. But if you use another man's sermon outline, give him credit. If you quote an especially good statement, document it. Integrity demands it—and you never know whether somebody in your congregation might own the same book!

If it is wrong to steal a man's material, it is also wrong to imitate his approach and style. "The style is the man" said Robert Frost, and he was right. Be yourself—your *best* self—and let the Holy Spirit put the imprint of your life on the message. If another man's message has blessed you, then allow it to permeate your own mind and heart so that you can make it your own and apply it to the people. Lay hold of the essentials, not the accidentals.

Be yourself and be true to yourself. That is the best kind of originality.

16. Strive for variety and balance.

Sameness leads to tameness. Predictable preaching is not powerful preaching.

We should vary our themes and diligently try to avoid "riding hobbies." Expository preaching through the books of the Bible usually results in a balanced diet for God's people. Vary your propositional sentences. They may take one of several forms:

> *Declarative:* "The Holy Spirit helps the believer."
>
> *Imperative:* "Every believer should be filled with the Holy Spirit of God."
>
> *Interrogative:* "How can we be filled with the Spirit?"
>
> *Hortatory:* "Keep on praying!"
>
> *Exclamatory:* "Just think of the joys of heaven!"
>
> *Definition:* "Faith means living without scheming."

Vary the development of the message. If

your outline is true to the text, then each development will follow the form of the text. Not every sermon should be an argument. If the passage is an argument, then that's the form it can take (although the imaginative preacher could deal with it in other ways). The "Magnificat" of Mary in Luke 1 is not of the same literary genre as Paul's defense in Acts 22. When a sermon is carefully prepared, it reflects the kind of material found in the text.

Vary the purposes of your sermons. Of course, there are *general* purposes to each sermon: winning the lost, encouraging the saved, reclaiming the fallen. But the *specific* aims ought to be varied from week to week, and they will be if the preacher is faithful in expounding the text. The preacher who forces his preconceived outline on a passage will lack balance and variety in his ministry. The preacher who permits the passage to speak for itself will be amazed at how much variety the Holy Spirit has written into the Bible.

17. Plan your preaching.

Spurgeon was able to prepare his Sunday
morning sermon on Saturday evening and his
Sunday evening sermon on Sunday after-
noon—but there are not many Spurgeons.
Most of us can make better use of our study
time if we know where we are going from
week to week. If the Spirit of God wants to
"break in" and give you a special message, he
is free to do so and nothing will be lost.

Just as each individual sermon must grow
out of the text, so the sermon series must
grow out of the context of the church and your
ministry to it. If you are growing in your own
spiritual life and in your knowledge of the
Bible, and if you are in touch with the Lord
and your people, God will guide you in your
planning. You may want to seek the counsel of
your spiritual leaders as well. Avoid artificial
series that look good on paper but have no
substance. Plan your congregation's spiritual

diet around solid nourishment from the Word.

Your preaching calendar will probably divide into these periods:

Labor Day to Thanksgiving

Advent season

New Year's Day to Ash Wednesday

Lenten season

Easter to Pentecost

Summer ministry

You need not observe the liturgical calendar to plan your preaching. These are simply suggested "time blocks" that may be used for sermon series. Dr. Andrew Blackwood has suggested that each season of the year have a different emphasis:

September to Christmas—undergirding

January to Easter—recruiting

Easter to Pentecost—instructing

Weeks after Pentecost—encouraging

These are broad categories, of course, because an element of each of these four ministries is found in almost every sermon.

Always plan a series before you announce it and start preaching it. This doesn't mean that each message must be in final form, but only that you have thought and prayed your way through the material, sketched out the messages, and feel confident with the approach. More than one preacher has been embarrassed in the middle of a series and either had to "bluff his way through" or simply stop. Like the man building the tower and the king going to war, we had better take inventory of our resources before we get started.

18. Sermons preached as part of a series must be independent and yet related.

Prepare each message as though it were the only one, and yet keep in mind that it is a part of a series. Consider the visitor who has not heard the previous messages, or the church member who heard but perhaps forgot what was said. Don't assume that your congregation will remember all that you have taught them; but, at the same time, don't spend too much time reviewing and reminding.

The pastor who starts off his message, "You will remember that last week we considered . . ." is asking most of his congregation to turn him off. The visitors didn't hear last week's sermon and the members have forgotten most of it. Let each message have a fresh introduction. Once you have gotten people's attention, you can relate your message to the others in the series; but even then, be careful not to demand too much.

Feel free to use ideas from previous messages, and don't always document them. Most people have to be reminded, and they appreciate the reminders!

Just as we must not tie our introduction to the previous message, neither should we tie the conclusion to the next message. You may not have the privilege of preaching the next message.

19. Preach to individuals.

A church accomplishes nothing; it is individuals in the church who get the job done. All effective speaking is to individuals. What the little girl said to her mother ought to be said by people who hear us: "Is Mr. Spurgeon speaking *to me?*"

This does not mean that the preacher must constantly be saying "you." There is nothing wrong with that approach, so long as we occasionally say "we" and "the church" (or some other synonym such as "God's people" or "believers"). If we prepare with individuals in mind—the representative people of our congregation with their representative needs—then we will have little difficulty preaching the Word in a personal way.

20. Never separate doctrine, duty, and devotion.

A sermon that explains Bible truth but makes no personal and practical application is only a theological lecture. At the same time, a sermon that exhorts and encourages Christian duty, without basing that duty on doctrine, could well be only a piece of religious propaganda. Likewise, a "devotional sermon" that aims only to "warm the heart" will do no lasting good if it has no doctrinal foundation or practical application.

The preacher aims at the heart (devotion), the mind (doctrine), and the will (duty). "Let them see clearly," said Phillips Brooks, "that you value no feeling which is not the child of truth and the father of duty" (*op. cit.*, p. 245). In most of Paul's epistles, he balanced doctrine

and duty; and we should follow his example.
Unless duty is based on doctrine—what Christ
has done for us—it becomes a burden; but
unless doctrine is tied to duty, it becomes
vague and impersonal.

The bridge between *learning* (doctrine)
and *living* (duty) is *loving:* "If ye love me,
keep my commandments" (John 14:15). "Do
not tell people how they ought to feel toward
Christ," wrote P. T. Forsythe. "Preach a Christ
that will make them feel as they ought."

Note how Paul related doctrine to duty:

Duty	*Doctrine*
giving	the grace of God— 2 Corinthians 8:1-9
forgiveness	God forgave you— Ephesians 4:32
speak truth	we belong to each other—Ephesians 4:25
walk in love	Christ loved us— Ephesians 5:1, 2
receive one another	Christ received us— Romans 15:7
don't judge each other	Christ is Lord— Romans 14:1-13

This is what it means to "preach Christ"—to relate all truth to his person and work. Effective preaching keeps the Savior preeminent in all things. Christ is not simply the message; he is also the motive.

21. Speak the truth in love.

Love makes truth palatable, while truth makes love practical. Truth without love could destroy a person by its brutality, while love without truth could destroy a person by its insincerity. Love without truth is sentimentality, feeling without responsibility. Truth without love is powerless to change lives, while love without truth could change them in the wrong direction.

It is not enough for the preacher to love the truth; he must also love the people to whom he ministers. "Preaching suffereth long and is kind; preaching envieth not; preaching vaunteth not itself, is not puffed up. . . ."

22. Have faith in preaching.

Preaching is a divinely appointed way to transmit God's truth. This does not minimize teaching, personal witnessing, or any other valid means of sharing the Word; but it does emphasize the importance of preaching. God had one Son and he was a preacher. "How shall they hear without a preacher?" (Rom. 10:14). Paul never tired of magnifying his preaching office. "Woe is unto me, if I preach not the gospel!" (1 Cor. 9:16).

The Word is seed and it takes time for it to germinate, grow, and produce fruit. Be patient; be prayerful. God's Word is never wasted. You may not see the harvest, but somebody else will; and God will be glorified.

23. Use your imagination.

Imagination is the faculty of making something new out of that which is old. All preachers say just about the same thing, if their preaching is at all biblical; but some say things in more interesting ways.

Imagination is not to be confused with fancy. The preacher must not strive to be clever and cute, but original. The preacher with imagination sees relationships between ancient truth and modern life. He sees into the heart of Scripture as well as into his own heart and the hearts of his listeners.

Creative preaching grows out of life and thought, and it is imagination that unites these two. Our preaching may be doctrinally and homiletically sound, and yet not worth listening to if it lacks imagination. The media people spend millions of dollars to create imaginative entertainment, and the manufacturers do the same to produce attractive products and packaging. The preacher ought to pay the price to develop his imagination and apply it to his preaching.

24. Preach a positive message.

While people do need to be warned, their greatest need is for positive teaching and direction. A highway sign that reads "This highway does not go to Los Angeles" is not much help. We want to know where the road *is* going.

Yes, some of the Ten Commandments are negative; but even they are based on Jehovah's first statement: "I am the Lord thy God!" We need the negative, but it must be strengthened by the positive. Negative preaching is discouraging to the listeners and does not promote true spiritual living. It can border on legalism.

25. Preach in the present tense.

It has well been said that nobody goes to church to find out what happened to the Jebusites. A sermon that lingers in the past tense is not really a sermon at all: it is either a Bible story or a lecture. We *live* in the present tense and we need to hear what God has to say to us *today*.

All Scripture is inspired and all Scripture is profitable. This means that there is a present-day message and application for each portion of the Word of God. It is the preacher's job to discover the timeless truths and principles that are in the Word, clothe them in understandable language, and apply them to the needs of a waiting congregation.

One writer noted that 2 Timothy 3:16 points the way for practical biblical preaching. The Word is profitable for *doctrine*—that's what is right; for *reproof*—that's what is not right; for *correction*—that's how to get right; and for *instruction in righteousness*—that's how to stay right.

The main points of your message must focus on life today and not on Moses, David, or Paul. What God did for the men and women of old, the heroes of faith, is meaningful to us today by way of warning (1 Cor. 10:1-12) and encouragement (Rom. 15:4). This includes the Old Testament, for, after all, that was the only Bible Jesus and the early church possessed. In their ministries, the apostles were able to give a modern, relevant message from the ancient Scriptures, and God blessed their words.

"He that hath an ear, let him hear what the Spirit saith unto the churches" (Rev. 2:7, 11, 17, 29; 3:6, 13, 22).

26. Never be satisfied with your preaching.

Once you are, nobody else will be. There is always more truth to learn from the Word, as well as more truth to live. We can always grow in our homiletical skills and in our presentation of the Word.

Success can become a great enemy of progress. Don't believe everything people say about your preaching.

When you find yourself cutting corners on your preparation because you think you have mastered all the skills, then stop and repent.

"I dread getting to be a mere preaching machine," said Spurgeon, "without my heart and soul being exercised in this solemn duty— lest it should be a mere piece of clock-work."

How, then, do we improve our preaching?

First, by cultivating our own spiritual life. The work that we do cannot be divorced from the life that we live. "Take heed unto thyself, and unto the doctrine . . ." was Paul's admonition to a young preacher.

Second, by constantly learning about preaching and all that relates to it. Not only must we read again the classic texts, but we must encounter the new books that are coming out, and seek to learn from them. Don't settle only for the writers who agree with you; read some that disagree with you. They may teach you more.

Third, by entering more fully into the lives of our people. We learn constantly from the book of humanity just as we learn from the Bible and the book of nature. The babies in the nursery, the children in school, the teenagers, the young singles, the newlyweds, the people in mid-life, and the senior saints will all enrich your life and your preaching. Whatever makes you more of a human being will help you become a better preacher, if you permit the Spirit to direct you.

Finally, by suffering in the will of God. Luther said that prayer, meditation, and suffering make a preacher, and he was right. The stars shine the brightest when the night is the darkest, and God is able to give us songs in the night.

II. Preaching Prohibitions

We have left undone those things which we ought to have done; and we have done those things which we ought not to have done.

The Book of Common Prayer
"A General Confession"

All of us have our list of things we wish preachers would not do. In fact, we have probably contributed to that list! We cannot cite chapter and verse to defend our opinions (or prejudices), but we like to think that the people in the pews would stand with us.

Here, then, are some of the sins preachers commit that we ought not commit.

1. Wasting time on long introductions to our sermons.

A preacher is like a man who hears a call for help and drops everything to run to the rescue. He is intent on one thing and he gives himself fully to it. But when he spends five or ten minutes getting into his sermon, he is like a man pausing to visit an art gallery before diving into the ocean to save the drowning swimmer.

The main purpose of the introduction is to create interest and convince the listener that he can be helped by hearing your message. The longer you wander around during the introduction, the easier it is for the listener to tune you out. On more than one occasion, we have found ourselves repressing the strong desire to shout, "For goodness' sake, start preaching! What, reverend sir, are you driving at?"

The chief time-wasters in the introduction are:

General comments about the weather, the congregation, the music, special guests, and even the announcements. If you feel constrained to discuss these inanities, do so before you stand up to preach. But keep in mind that every minute you waste early in the service will rob you of preaching time.

Comments about the sermon itself. Some preachers don't seem to understand that we don't want to hear *about* the sermon; we want to hear the sermon.

Jokes. While humor has its place in preaching, a completely unrelated piece of humor is hardly the best way to open a message from God's Word. It is a mystery to us why some preachers think they must always tell a joke before they read their text and preach the message. When there is a hostile audience or an atmosphere of tension, perhaps a bit of humor can help to change that atmosphere; but certainly this is an exception. Can you imagine Peter telling a joke before he preached at Pentecost, or Paul entertaining the philosophers on Mars' Hill?

References to last week's sermon. (See #18 in the first part of this book.) Here sits a man with a broken heart and a problem-filled life. He came to church hoping to get some help from God's Word. The choir has sung and the song helped prepare him for the message. The preacher opens his mouth and says, "Now, you'll recall that last week—or was it two weeks ago?—we discussed the first six verses of this chapter." Instantly our needy visitor says, "Well, I should have come last week . . . but maybe there's still hope." Instead of the preacher getting to the point, he tries to summarize three weeks of preaching; and by that time, our friend isn't listening anymore.

It is our feeling that most of the people who come to church want to hear from God and there is no need for the preacher to spend a great deal of time getting their attention. Without being abrupt, he can state the intent of the message through his propositional sentence.

Here are some examples of effective introductions:

> *"He ascended into heaven." Did He? Where is heaven? What is it? Is it a place? Can we know what it is or where it is?*
>
> —G. A. Studdert-Kennedy

Once more on Christmas Sunday morning we come to the church to celebrate the Christ. But which Christ? Anyone reading what is afoot in books and magazines today can observe that two Christs are in the minds of men—the Christ of history and the Christ of experience.

—Harry Emerson Fosdick

It is a common notion that anybody can sing. Why can you sing? Why, because I have been taught. That is your mistake. You can sing mechanically, exactly, properly, with the right time, right tune, but really and truly you cannot sing.

—Joseph Parker, on Isaiah 50:4

I do not think there is a word in the English language so little understood as the word Gospel.

—Dwight L. Moody

There is a two-fold solemnity which belongs to the dying hour—it is the winding up of life, and it is the commencement of eternity.

—Frederick W. Robertson

2. Basing our sermons on suppositions instead of Scripture.

We once heard a moving Communion address based on the assumption that Barabbas came to the cross and was so moved by what he saw that he trusted Christ and was converted. Apart from the fact that this borders on the "moral influence theory" of the atonement, there is the additional problem of the absence of biblical proof. Surely if Barabbas had been saved, something would have been said either in Scripture or in church history.

People do not come to church to hear what we imagine. They come to hear what we know God has said in his Word. There are so many wonderful divine certainties in Scripture that it borders on blasphemy for a preacher to base his sermon on suppositions and assumptions.

" "The prophet who has a dream may relate his dream, but let him who has My word speak My word in truth. What does straw have in common with grain?' declares the Lord" (Jer. 23:28, NASB).

3. Using poor English and bad grammar.

Words are the preacher's only tools and he must be skilled in using them. Yet we hear supposedly educated preachers saying things such as, "God did this for you and I," or, "What a blessing it was to she and I." We know that this is the way many people speak today, but that doesn't make it correct. Do not "follow a multitude" in doing wrong... (Exodus 23:2).

Slang and various kinds of jargon have no place in the pulpit unless they are used in quotation or to illustrate a point that cannot be illustrated any other way. And while we are on the subject, we shall include a few words about cliches, evangelical and otherwise: *avoid them.* Cliches are the "small change" of communications, and they don't enrich the sermon very much, especially for thinking people. Good preaching, like good writing, is clear, crisp, uncluttered, and easy to understand.

Every preacher ought to read books about words and good writing. Here are a few to consider:

> *On Writing Well,* by William Zinsser
>   (Harper & Row)
> *The Art of Plain Talk,* by Rudolf Flesch
>   (Harper)
> *Strictly Speaking* and *A Civil Tongue,* by
>   Edwin Newman (Bobbs-Merrill)
> *On Language,* and *What's the Good
>   Word,* by William Safire *(Times* Books)
> *The Writer's Art,* by James J. Kilpatrick
>   (Andrews, McMeel & Parker, Inc.)

If you need a review course in grammar, start with *The Elements of Style* by Strunk and White (Macmillan).

4. Hiding behind the pulpit.

If you have a problem with somebody in your church family, obey Matthew 18:15-17 and settle the matter privately. But please don't carry your personal complaints into the pulpit to make them a part of the sermon. This includes hints about your salary. Why rob the entire congregation of the blessing of the Word so you can vent your feelings, and, from your secure ecclesiastical bunker, attack your enemy? Shame on you!

5. Preaching everything we think we know.

The beginning preacher makes this mistake more often than the experienced one. Fresh out of school, he is so enamored of his notes that he tries to transform them into sermon outlines, and his congregation is subjected to terms such as *logos, hypostatic union, parousia,* and so on. We know of one church, located near a seminary, which always knew what the new student pastor would preach about in his first sermon—the *logos* doctrine in John 1. Why? Because that was one of the first lectures given in the Greek class each year.

Your seminary notes are to your sermons what the list of nutrients is to the food in the box; but people need food, not an analysis of the food. This rule applies to the preaching of an entire book of the Bible. It takes a skilled preacher to cover an entire book and not leave the congregation lost in the details. New Testament Survey notes are not sermon notes.

Digest your material first, then prepare messages that meet human needs and glorify Jesus Christ.

6. Using illustrations carelessly.

The purpose of an illustration is to make the truth clearer to the listener, or to apply the truth to the heart so that the will can respond. Using a story simply "for effect" or "for laughs" is unpardonable.

Be sure all illustrations are pertinent and are not simply "dropped in" to fill up the outline.

Be sure they are accurate. Check the original sources and verify the facts.

Be sensitive to the people in your congregation. If someone has recently lost a loved one by suicide, try to avoid using a "suicide story" just to make a point. You may only deepen wounds that desperately need healing.

Never base your sermon on an illustration, no matter how good the story might be. Base your message on the Word.

Never, NEVER relate as your own an illustration from the life of another person. It is dishonest and it could be embarrassing as well. Somebody listening might know the truth about the story.

Avoid books of illustrations. The stories are old, some of them are inaccurate, and other preachers are using them. There are scores of worn-out illustrations that ought to be buried with honor, but, alas, they keep showing up in books and sermons. Don't let them show up in your messages. Strive to be original.

7. Overpowering people with our vocabulary.

Preach to express, not to impress. Preach to be understood. It has well been said that the man who shoots above his target does not prove that he has better ammunition, but only that he cannot shoot.

Sometimes the message requires the use of theological terms, so take time to explain and illustrate them. But avoid "dropping in" words and phrases that your people do not understand. You will only encourage them to stop listening. "It must have been a great sermon," said one parishioner; "I didn't understand a word of it!" Impressed—but not helped. The time was wasted.

Avoid the temptation to show off your learning. Great teachers and preachers speak so as to be understood. This especially applies to references to Hebrew and Greek. Don't give grammar lectures or drown the congregation in "cognates." One minister based a funeral message on the meaning of the Greek word *parakaleō*, and used the word repeatedly. The mourners were not impressed—or comforted.

When you introduce Greek or Hebrew words or terms, use your imagination in presenting them. "The soldiers in Paul's congregation would have recognized this word . . ." or, "The people in Ephesus who received this letter would understand the meaning of this word Paul wrote. . . ." Most Greek and Hebrew theological terms are beautiful "picture words" and should not be defaced by technical clutter that builds up the preacher's ego but tears down the sermon's effectiveness.

8. Delivering the message carelessly.

How we deliver the message is important. The content of the message may be the arrowhead that will pierce the heart, but the feathers on the arrow represent the delivery of the message so that it reaches its target. We preachers can learn a great deal from effective public speakers and actors who know how to "deliver the goods."

To change the metaphor, if the sermon is the meal, then our delivery is the way we serve the meal so that the listener wants to "take it in."

Don't assume a "pulpit style" that is different from your normal style of conversation and communication. Don't imitate some other preacher; be yourself—your best self.

Preach to the people. Look at them. Don't address your message to the back wall or the ceiling; preach to the congregation.

Preaching is not performing, nor is the pulpit a stage or the congregation an audience. Since the preacher is a part of the message, he had better be the same person in the pulpit as he is out of the pulpit.

Good delivery does not attract attention to itself. It is simply a tool, wisely used, to get the truth of the Word into the hearts of people.

It may take a few years, but work to discover and develop the preaching style that is best for you, and then stick to it. There is always room for improvement, so don't get careless.

9. Concluding sermons with vague generalities.

If Peter at Pentecost had preached as some of us do, when the people cried out, "Men and brethren, what shall we do?" he would have said rather apologetically:

"Well, let me review my main points for you again . . . and you really need to deal with your sins . . . and whatever the Lord says to you, do it. . . ." But Peter knew what he was aiming at before he started! He knew his commission and that determined his conclusion.

Strictly speaking, the conclusion of the sermon ought to be prepared first. As you study the text and prepare the message, you must keep in mind what it is you are trying to accomplish. Remember that the purpose of a sermon is not to explain a subject but to achieve an object.

Whenever you hear any of the following

"conclusions," you can be assured that the preacher did not prepare:

> *May the Lord bless these few thoughts from his Word, and may all of us obey what his Spirit says to the churches.*

> *Well, our time is up, so let's pause to pray.*

> *Now, let's review the main points again before we have the benediction and go to our various homes.*

> *Oh, there is so much more I could say! But I trust these truths have been a blessing to your heart.*

Can you imagine a salesman winding up his sales presentation with such nebulous talk? If he did, he would be broke—and fired.

If the message you prepared has spoken to your own heart (and it had better), then you can apply it to the hearts and lives of the people who hear you. Be specific. Call for a verdict. Challenge the people to respond. You may not see that response immediately, but ultimately you will.

If your propositional sentence is what it

ought to be, you will know what it is you want
God to do in the lives of your people. A vague
proposition leads to a vague conclusion—and
vague blessings.

10. Hopping rapidly from verse to verse in the Bible.

There is nothing wrong with using several verses to support a point, but let's give our people time to hear and locate the references. Not everybody will turn to each reference, but each listener has the right to hear the reference and the verse and let it sink in before he is asked to consider another one. Some preachers use a homiletical machine gun and spray the congregation with Bible bullets until the listeners are inwardly crying out for mercy.

Most of the people who listen to us preach don't spend many hours in Bible reading or Bible study. Some, unfortunately, never pick up the Bible from one Sunday to another. Young believers have a difficult time finding the different books of the Bible. If it is important to your message that you refer to several passages, at least give the people time to locate them. Better still, why not list the verses in the bulletin so they can read them on their own?

11. Constantly changing translations.

We thought that the translation explosion was over, but it seems to be getting louder; and each new translation must have its own "study edition" as well. As a result, the local church family is perhaps the only class that comes to school without a uniform textbook.

Each believer needs to find that translation that best suits him, that speaks to his heart, and then stick with it. The reading of a new translation does not guarantee spiritual growth. Likewise, each local church probably ought to decide on one "pew Bible" and use it, no matter what the individual members may do personally. Visitors may be confused by the multiplicity of versions and feel left out when the Bible they hold in their hands is different from the one being used in the pulpit.

The preacher who preaches from the Authorized Version one week, the Revised Standard the next week, and perhaps a modern paraphrase the third week is making good use of his library but bad use of his opportunity. Decide on one translation and use it.

12. Betraying confidences in our preaching.

The Scottish lady who, while dying, said to her pastor, "Now, don't you go and make a story out of me!" knew the weakness of the minister. For some reason, we like to parade in public some things that ought to remain private.

"Just this past week," announces the brave pastor, "one of our members told me that he had been unfaithful to his wife." The result? Every woman starts to suspect her husband, every husband begins to despise the pastor, and the whole congregation determines never to go to him for personal counsel.

If told in a guarded way, experiences you have had away from your church family may be used constructively in a sermon; but keep in mind that people do have friends and relatives in other places. If a pastor wants his people to trust him, then he had better not open up his counseling records in public. Nor should he use experiences from other pastors that he knows. News travels fast, and loose lips sink ships—and ministries.

It is a blessed thing to have the confidence of your good people. All of us can learn from the mother who asked her pediatrician, "How can I keep the confidence of my child?" The wise doctor replied, "Never lose it." People want to trust their pastor. Let's give them every reason to believe that they can.

13. Abusing the use of humor in the pulpit.

If the preacher has a sense of humor, he had better dedicate it to the Lord and let the Spirit direct him in its use. For true humor can become a toy to play with, a tool to build with, or a dangerous weapon to fight with.

Since the whole man must be in the pulpit, the preacher dare not lay aside a part of his God-given personality. Charles Spurgeon was once criticized for his humor in the pulpit; and his only reply was that his critics ought to know how much humor he suppressed! If they knew, they would think more highly of him!

Preaching is serious business, and the preacher must not stoop to become a comedian. Particularly, he must never joke about eternal things. We wonder how many bereaved people have been deeply hurt by careless preachers telling tasteless jokes about death and funerals. There is a place for wit and subtle humor in the pulpit, but there is no place for comedy, for what Phillips Brooks called "the clerical jester."

Humor is meant to be a means to an end. It is the spice that makes the meal more palatable, the sugar that helps the medicine go down. A flash of wit can help to relieve tension or overcome opposition. It can regain the attention of a sleepy congregation, or prepare the way for a final thrust of the sword of the Spirit. Humor is not the arrowhead; it is the feather that helps the shaft hit the mark.

If humor is not natural to the preacher, then he had better forget about it. We have heard some humorless preachers ruin their own messages—and create some embarrassing situations—because they thought they had to be funny. Be yourself, your *best* self.

"I must confess that I would rather hear people laugh," said Spurgeon, "than I would see them asleep in the house of God; and I would rather get the truth into them through the medium of ridicule than I would have it neglected, or leave the people to perish through lack of reception of the message."

In the pulpit, humor must be either a tool to

build with or a weapon to fight with, but never a toy to play with. We have thirty minutes in which to raise the dead. We have no time for toys.

14. Preaching ourselves instead of the Word.

The preacher is definitely a part of the message, since God communicates his truth through human personality; but the preacher must not be the theme of the message. Whenever he speaks of himself and his experiences with God, he must do so in order to serve the people and magnify the Savior.

"For we preach not ourselves, but Christ Jesus the Lord; and ourselves your servants for Jesus' sake" (2 Cor. 4:5).

Both in his writings and in his sermons, Paul talked about himself and shared his personal feelings and experiences; but it was always with the goal of exalting Jesus Christ and illustrating his work of grace in Paul's life. This is a good model to follow.

Some preachers talk about themselves so much, you could reconstruct their lives from their sermons. Others are so private that their personal experiences are told as anonymous anecdotes. Both extremes should be avoided. The congregation wants to see Christ, but they want to see him through the ministry of a real person, even one who occasionally makes mistakes.

Taking Inventory of the Message

1. Is the message solidly based on Scripture?
2. Does it exalt the Person and work of Jesus Christ?
3. Will it meet the needs of people?
4. Is the theme a timeless truth worth talking about?
5. Is the message organized so that I can preach it clearly and the people understand it easily? Is there a concise and clear statement of purpose? Is there a clear plan of development? Is there practical application that makes the message personal?
6. Are all Scripture references and historical facts accurate?
7. Is the message real to me personally so that I may make it real to others?

8. Does this message fit into the total "preaching plan" for this church and into the context of the church's ministry at this time?
9. Does the message fit into the ministry of the Church at large and Christ's concern to save a lost world?
10. Is the message worth preaching again?

So, What's Cooking?

Behold, a cook went forth to cook. And as he cooked, his household was nourished and satisfied, so much so that they went out into the highways and hedges and brought in the hungry and thirsty, and the house was filled.

But it came to pass one day that the cook discovered a cookbook. In this cookbook were recipes and menus, and also analytical charts explaining the nutrition in various foods. There were also beautiful pictures of succulent dishes.

"I will now step aside and examine this great book," said the cook. "It must have great value, for it was published by a cooking school that trained the three greatest cooks in the land."

So, he read in the book day by day, while feeding his household leftovers. He became so excited about the menus, charts, and pictures,

that he wanted to share them with his household.

"My household is too large for all of them to
see this book," he said to himself. "What shall I
do? I know what I shall do! I shall purchase an
overhead projector and thus enable everyone
to benefit from the wealth of material in this
cookbook."

So, he purchased a projector and began at
each meal to explain where food came from,
what it contains, and how it can be prepared.
His household became engrossed in the charts
and pictures. Before long, they began to bring
notebooks and pencils to the table instead of
knives and forks. But by then, all the leftovers
were gone and the cook had not prepared any
new meals. The household spent their time
doing nothing but discussing some new menu
or analytical chart.

And it came to pass that the household
started to become weak and grow thin. Yea,
the cook himself began to lose weight so that
he could no longer carry his overhead projector to the dining room. "I will make myself a
dish such as I used to make," he said to himself. And he did. As the aroma of the meal
wafted through the house, the family gathered
at the table as before, but this time they came

with their knives and forks. Soon it was like old times again, as they ate and were nourished. The cook had great joy as he saw the family gain weight and grow in strength.

And he said to himself, "Yea, this may be a fine book, but it is no substitute for a good meal. My household cannot thrive on menus, recipes, pictures, and the chemical analyses of the food. I will arise and go to my kitchen and spend my time preparing dishes that will feed my family."

And he did; and the cookbook gathered dust on the shelf, while in the bookstores, it was selling like hotcakes.

EUTYCHUS X